Original title:
Echoes of Elmwood

Copyright © 2025 Creative Arts Management OÜ
All rights reserved.

Author: Adrian Caldwell
ISBN HARDBACK: 978-1-80567-324-8
ISBN PAPERBACK: 978-1-80567-623-2

Rooted Footsteps of Forgotten Souls

In the grove where shadows play,
Lost shoes giggle, come what may.
A squirrel dances, prancing bold,
While secrets of the past unfold.

Under branches, hats are tossed,
Laughter echoes, tempers crossed.
A frog leaps high in tree-top style,
As ghosts recall their days gone wild.

Harmony of Laughter in the Leaves

Leaves rustle with a mischievous cheer,
Whispers of joy that all can hear.
A raccoon juggles nuts with flair,
While chattering birds send giggles in the air.

Rabbits hop to a forgotten tune,
Dancing 'neath the watchful moon.
The breeze carries laughter, light and free,
An orchestra of nature's jubilee.

The Enigma of Evening's Embrace

The sun dips down with a teasing grin,
Fireflies sparkle, let the fun begin.
Crickets chirp their secret song,
To the rhythm where the misfits belong.

Shadows stretch with a coy delight,
As owls chuckle through the night.
Mischief brews in the twilight glow,
A riddle that the wise may know.

Cycles of Change in the Canopy

Branches sway in a playful dance,
As leaves continue their silly prance.
The seasons shift, but joy remains,
In laughter-filled drops from gentle rains.

Flowers giggle, their colors bright,
Winking at bees in pure delight.
The maple's chuckle, the oak's delight,
In the circle of life, all feels just right.

Eternal Embers of Evergreens

In a forest of thoughts so bright,
The squirrels hold a raucous flight.
They giggle and chatter, what a sight,
Chasing shadows till the night.

Old trees whisper tales of yore,
Of acorn armies and nuts galore.
The pinecones roll, who could ignore?
Nature's jesters, forever more.

A bear appears with a tutu on,
Dancing with glee from dusk till dawn.
In this kingdom, who's the con?
The laughter lasts when he's all gone.

So join the jest in this great glade,
Where laughter and mirth will never fade.
Among the trees where fun is laid,
In this woodland party, be unafraid.

Veils of Vines and Vehement Vistas

Amidst the vines where the green twirls,
Lies a frog who believes he's pearls.
He croaks for fame, his voice unfurls,
In the bog, he's king of swirls.

The rabbits wear hats and prance,
Throwing a dance and a curious glance.
Playing hopscotch, they take a chance,
In the meadow, they find romance.

A windswept breeze causes a ruckus,
A kite caught in branches, oh what a fuss!
The children laugh, "Look at that plus!"
In this wild world, joy's never thus.

So join the revels where whimsy's the norm,
In the world of vines, where oddities swarm.
Let's revel together, away from the storm,
In laughter's embrace, we find our form.

Whispers Beneath the Canopy

Under the leaves, squirrels debate,
Who stole the acorn, oh what a fate!
Chirping birds laugh, oh what a scene,
As chipmunks march, a little less keen.

These woodland secrets, a riotous play,
Mice hosting dances by light of day.
Branching out loudly, the branches do sway,
Nature's comedy, we're all on display.

Shadows of the Forgotten Grove

A raccoon named Larry thinks he's a star,
Wearing a hat made from trash—oh, bizarre!
He struts through the trees like a champion bold,
While owls shake their heads, their wisdom untold.

The trees whisper tales of dance floor fables,
Where beetles rock out on the old fallen tables.
Each giggle and burst, from branches to stream,
In this hidden spot, where nothing's as it seems.

Secrets Carried by the Breeze

The wind tells stories with a cheeky twist,
Of a gallivanting frog who can't resist.
He jumps high and low, with grace it seems,
Chasing after laughter, in his wild dreams.

Leaves tickle the branches, creating a fuss,
As snails spin tales, without any rush.
With giggles of flora, a party unfolds,
In this realm of whimsy, nothing's too bold.

Lament of the Old Trees

With bark that's wrinkled like an old wise sage,
The trees swap their jokes, oh, they're all the rage!
Beneath their strong limbs, a jest or two,
"Did you hear the one about the wild kangaroo?"

They chuckle and creak, in the soft, sunny light,
Retelling their tales through the deep of the night.
A comedy show where the roots dig deep,
In this wooded laughter, we joyfully leap.

Dreams Drenched in Dew

In the morning light, we trip over dreams,
Frogs croak symphonies, or so it seems.
The grass tickles toes, a curious tease,
While the sun yawns big, like a sleepy breeze.

Mice whisper secrets in a rustling hush,
Squirrels play tag in a wild little rush.
A dog licks the dew from his favorite tree,
While a cat in a sunbeam pretends to be free.

Distant Drumming of Woodpeckers

Knock, knock, says the woodpecker so spry,
As he hammers on dreams that flutter by.
What's he building? Perhaps a joke or two,
Or a tiny condo for squirrels in blue.

The trees chuckle softly, their branches sway,
As the pecker's beat counts out the day.
Neighbors peek out for a laugh to unfold,
At the antics of woodpecker, brave and bold.

The Gentle Language of Leaves

Leaves gossip softly in their green attire,
With whispers of winds that never tire.
A butterfly quips, 'Did you see that dance?'
As they flutter and spin, lost in a trance.

The maple snickers, 'I pranked the old oak!'
'Told him he'd fall—such a back-breaking joke!'
They shimmer bright with laughter at dusk,
While fireflies blink in the cool evening musk.

The Spirit of the Swaying Birch

The birch does a jig in the warm summer air,
While the grass rolls its eyes, like it just doesn't care.
'Take it easy, friend! You're swaying too much,'
Said the shy little dandelion, cringing with touch.

Bees buzz a tune that the clouds can't ignore,
As the birch shakes its roots, wanting to score.
It's a party of nature, full of joy and cheer,
Where every twig dances, and laughter draws near.

The Memory of Fallen Acorns

Once bright acorns took a dive,
They tumble down, oh what a jive!
With squirrels dancing, oh so spry,
Who knew they'd give a chance to fly?

In autumn's breeze, they roll and spin,
A nutty race where all can win.
The laughter rings, it knows no bounds,
As critters play on leaf-strewn grounds.

Ghosts of the Ancient Trunks

The trees remembered tales of yore,
Old socks and hats hung by the door.
With knots and gnarls, they start to chat,
"Remember when we wore that hat?"

A ghostly laugh from hollow bark,
Whispers of sweet piquant park.
They giggle loud at silly things,
From acorn fights to treehouse swings.

Hushed Voices in the Glade

In twilight's glow, the shadows jest,
Two rabbits argue who's the best.
"Hop with style!" one cries in glee,
While the other thumps, "I disagree!"

A chorus of crickets chime along,
Adding beats to their hopping song.
With whispers soft, the foxes tease,
As night wraps all in playful ease.

Reverie Beneath the Green Veil

Under the leaves, where laughter grows,
A tale of stumbles and silly toes.
The deer trip lightly, whoops abound,
As they prance through soft leafy ground.

Beneath the boughs, the fun won't cease,
In nature's dance, they find their peace.
With giggles blending, joy is clear,
In the green shade, they shed their fear.

Vestiges of Sunlight at Dusk

The sun takes a bow, with a wink and a grin,
As shadows play tag, let the games begin.
A squirrel on a branch, doing a dance,
While crickets are laughing, lost in a trance.

The grass starts to giggle, tickled by beams,
As fireflies sparkle, like wacky dreams.
The breeze steals a laugh, with a mischievous sway,
Bringing the sunlight to join in the play.

The old oak tree chuckles, its knobby arms raised,
At the folly of twilight, so absurd yet praised.
With every bright moment, the humor takes flight,
As daylight surrenders, to the joys of the night.

The Language of Rustling Foliage

Leaves whisper secrets, gossip with flair,
A rustle, a chuckle, floating in air.
Branches high five as the wind breezes by,
While ants in a line practice their dance, oh my!

The bushes break up in a fit of high squeaks,
As squirrels in hats show their acrobatic peaks.
A flower sings silly, 'Look at me, look!'
While the bushes all chuckle, it's quite the fine nook.

In every strange rustle, stories take flight,
Of ticklish old trees in the soft golden light.
Nature's own comedy, a stage so grand,
With every fun twist, a slapstick band.

Whispers in the Willows

Willows lean in, sharing a laugh,
As ducks quack a joke on the old wooden raft.
The pond joins the fun, with splashes of cheer,
While frogs cracking puns croak loud and clear.

The breeze tickles leaves, making a fuss,
While the giggling grasses all join the ruckus.
A heartbeat of humor beats under the boughs,
While fireflies flash on their light-up brows.

Mirthful old willows, with roots deep in jest,
Grow weary of whispers, they just need some rest.
But as night thickens cozy, the laughter stays,
In this woodland theater, nature always plays.

Shadows Beneath the Canopy

Shadows peek out with a grin, oh so sly,
While hushed giggles echo, as breezes drift by.
A raccoon plays peek-a-boo, hiding with glee,
In the winks of the twilight, as silly as can be.

Under green umbrellas where mysteries dwell,
The ferns throw a party — can you hear the bell?
With each rustle and laugh, the woods come alive,
In a comedy caper where the shadows contrive.

Every flicker of light holds a chuckle inside,
As nocturnal friends gather, a hilarious ride.
This patchwork of shadows with mischief unfurls,
Under the giggling canopy, joy twirls and swirls.

A Lullaby for Wandering Shadows

In the moonlight, shadows dance,
Whispering secrets in a prance.
A squirrel juggles acorns high,
While fireflies twinkle in the sky.

A raccoon croons a silly tune,
To sleepy owls beneath the moon.
The wind joins in with a gentle hum,
As branches sway, they all succumb.

The night wears laughter like a cloak,
While trees giggle with every joke.
A badger snorts with glee so bold,
As tales of mischief do unfold.

So let the shadows roam and play,
In the night, they find their way.
With giggles stacked and whispers bright,
They frolic under starry light.

The Canopy's Quiet Chronicles

In branches high, the whispers flow,
Tales of antics, soft and low.
A parrot paints the world so bright,
While chattering squirrels take to flight.

A wandering snail in his slow climb,
Forgets the rush, takes his sweet time.
The owls hoot at a missed chance,
As the raccoons join in a wacky dance.

Mushrooms giggle beneath their hats,
As ants march on in silly spats.
The breeze carries scents of sweet pie,
While bees buzz tunes that make you sigh.

Underneath the leafy embrace,
Every creature finds their place.
In laughter thick and hearts so free,
The canopy hums its symphony.

Whispers from the Woodland

Beneath the leaves, a rabbit sneezes,
The forest chuckles, it never ceases.
Mice in coats are playing chess,
While trees gossip without distress.

A chipmunk learns to juggle nuts,
But drops them all—oh, such a klutz!
The daisies sway, they find it grand,
As laughter rings through the soft land.

A dandelion thinks it's a star,
Winks at the moon from afar.
The brook giggles as it flows,
With stories of where the wild wind blows.

In every rustle, a joke lingers,
As foxes tell tales with sly fingers.
In this wood, the light shines bright,
With whispers that make the heart feel light.

The Enchanted Grove's Serenade

In the grove where fervor sways,
A frog rehearses for its plays.
With every ribbit, a laugh breaks free,
As the willow weeps in harmony.

Bugs in tuxedos on a stroll,
Debating which flower plays the role.
A snappy snail steals the stage,
In this leafy world, they turn the page.

A chorus of crickets hums a tune,
While mushrooms sway like little balloons.
The winds bring giggles from afar,
In this enchanted grove bizarre.

So come, join in, let laughter ring,
For in this grove, the night is king.
With rhythms wild and spirits gay,
We dance and laugh, come what may.

Resplendent Revelries in the Green

Beneath the boughs we danced with glee,
The squirrels looked on, not quite carefree.
With laughter loud, we spilled our drinks,
While birds nearby exchanged their winks.

A picnic spread with nibbles galore,
And ants held parties on the forest floor.
The flowers chuckled in colors bright,
As we tripped over roots, what a sight!

Laughter rang out like chimes in air,
As we flopped on grass without a care.
The sun peeked through in playful rays,
While we basked here for lazy days.

So here's to merriment, jokes, and zest,
In our leafy haven, we are truly blessed.

Paths Aligned Beneath the Stars

Under twinkling lights, we made our way,
With mismatched socks in a humorous display.
We bumped into branches, oh what a spree,
How trees must giggle when it's just you and me.

We whispered secrets to the night so clear,
While crickets croaked like a house band near.
Each shadow twirled, in its silly dance,
As we stumbled and twirled, lost in a trance.

A moonlit game of hide and seek,
As owls hooted laughter—they're quite the cheek!
The stars were guides, but we missed our cues,
Falling over grass, sharing nightly blues.

Yet we embraced that whimsical plight,
And painted our stories in the still of night.

The Timeless Tale of Twilit Trees

Once upon a time in a dreamy glade,
Where trees told tales that never would fade.
They'd shake their leaves when tickled by breeze,
And offer up shade for us if you please.

Each trunk a storyteller, wood gnarled and wise,
With knots and grooves like ancient ties.
We sat at their roots, trying not to snore,
As they spun wild yarns of war and of lore.

But sometimes their stories, they went off the track,
About woodland creatures who wore tiny hats.
With acorns as crowns and moss for their shoes,
We burst into laughter, oh, what a ruse!

Yet in the twilight, we'd listen and grin,
Grateful for tales that made our heads spin.

Fading Footsteps through Flora

Through wildflowers popping, we ventured along,
With every misstep came a new silly song.
We squished through mud, leaving footprints so wide,
Like wild little ducks who refuse to abide.

Each plant had a story to share as we passed,
With whispers of grass about memories amassed.
The daisies giggled, the dandelions sighed,
As we wobbled and bobbled, bumped and we tried.

We'd trip over roots while crafting our rhyme,
With the sun setting low, it felt like a crime.
Yet laughter lit paths where shadows took flight,
Dancing with blooms in the soft fading light.

So we wove through the flora with steps full of cheer,
Creating a carnival as nature drew near.

Echoes of a Wistful Wind

The breeze whispered secrets, oh so sly,
Tickling the trees and making them sigh.
A squirrel danced, acorns took flight,
As leaves laughed along, what a sight!

In the park, a balloon met a tree,
"Don't pop me!" it begged, with glee.
A shadow of a dog raced for fun,
But landed on the grass, his day's work done!

A picnic basket rolled, plotting its course,
Chasing those ants, with mighty force.
Sandwiches giggled, then took a leap,
While soda cans burped, it was quite the heap!

As twilight drew close, the fun wouldn't cease,
A playful wind danced, spinning in peace.
And oh, what a party this garden could host,
Cheers to the antics, we love the most!

In the Company of Crickets

At twilight's first call, the crickets convene,
Throwing a bash with a raucous routine.
Some chirp like opera stars on the stage,
While others freestyle, let loose their rage!

A mouse joins the fray, in search of a snack,
While fireflies twinkle, lighting the track.
"Hey, is that cheese?" the critters all cheer,
As someone yells, "Save some for me, dear!"

An owl hoots loudly, declaring a break,
While ants bring out treats, for goodness' sake!
The night stretches on, laughter in tune,
As shadows shimmy beneath the bright moon.

With each little chirp, bonds begin to grow,
In this raucous gathering, joy starts to flow.
For who needs a band when you've got the night?
In the company of crickets, all feels just right!

Ramblings of Wayward Wildflowers

A daisy once dreamt she could dance on the breeze,
"Oh, look at me!" she shouted with ease.
The tulips just giggled, a well-mannered laugh,
As a dandelion, bold, plotted her path!

Petals turned pages in sunshine's great book,
"We seek adventure!" one flower said, took
A step to the left, then a hop to the right,
While a buttercup blushed in the warm, golden light.

A bee zipped on by, trying to steer clear,
Of petals that danced with wild, joyful cheer.
"Just a quick pollination!" he buzzed with a grin,
But found himself caught in their whirlpool spin!

As twilight descended, the flowers stood proud,
Crowning the fields, whispering loud.
In their merry chaos, the wildflowers found,
That laughter brings color to life all around.

Sunsets Over Silent Sylvan

The sun draped her gown, a bright orange glow,
While shadows got silly, all moving in tow.
Rabbits played tag, with a flip and a bound,
As they dashed through the thicket, joyfully found.

Beneath leafy arches, the laughter rolled wide,
As squirrels, oh so crafty, skittered with pride.
They plotted to pilfer a young bird's last seed,
Thinking, "We'll feast with all joyful speed!"

A frog croaked a tune, an odd serenade,
While all of the critters danced in the glade.
"I'm the best crooner; let's hear your best riff!"
While the trees rolled their eyes at the noisy old stiff.

With the dusk drawing near, and stars on display,
The woodland brigade laughed the night all away.
Unplanned, they discovered, within nature's sweet space,
Life's funny antics leave smiles on each face!

Past Lives Under the Skylight

Old shoes left by the door,
Prancing mice, asking for more.
Ghosts of laughter tickle the air,
With each tale, we pull up a chair.

Chairs that creak like an old joke,
Whispers of breezes, the trees spoke.
A cat on the roof, juggling hats,
Murmuring secrets to curious rats.

Once a pirate, a dog in disguise,
Chasing a squirrel that danced in the skies.
Now they reminisce, like old pals,
Trading their stories with tea and pals.

Under skylights where dreams collide,
Memories bounce, in giggles they hide.
Every flicker, a moment to share,
In the laughter, we float without care.

Notes of Nature's Nostalgia

The trees hum tunes of the past,
While a frog breaks into song, oh what a blast!
Flowers sway to nature's own beat,
As bees join in with a wiggly retreat.

A squirrel recites its funny rhyme,
Saying acorns fall, all in good time.
The brook chuckles with gentle glee,
A tap-dancing snail, as spry as can be.

Old whispers float in the breeze so light,
While butterflies twirl in a joyful flight.
Nature chuckles at all of our plans,
While painting the world with fancy hands.

Notes of nostalgia bounce from the trees,
While laughter drifts lightly along with the breeze.
In this playful symphony, we find our dreams,
Each chuckle echoing like sunlit beams.

The Unseen Dances of Dew

Dewdrops leap in the morning light,
As spiders weave webs, what a sight!
In the grass, tiny disco balls,
While sleepy flowers stretch and sprawl.

A ladybug twirls, wearing her hat,
As the bumblebees join in with a pat.
Each petal shakes in a quirky way,
While the sun peeks in to start the day.

The wind laughs, stirring leaves so bright,
As petals giggle in their delight.
A parade of ants begins to groove,
In nature's dance, they find their move.

With each drop, a secret revealed,\nNature's quirks humorously concealed.
In the unseen, joy sprinkles through,
A delightful show with every dew.

Voices of the Verdant Vale

Whispers wander through the green,
Tickling the ferns that smile and preen.
While capricious clouds play tag in the sky,
A jolly parrot sings 'Oh my, oh my!'

Mushrooms gossip, high tea they hold,
As squirrels tell tales both silly and bold.
The soft grass grumbles, 'What's the next game?'
Each sound here dances, without any shame.

A brook babbles, sharing its dreams,
With fish too busy plotting their schemes.
And up on a branch, an old owl yawns,
Says, 'Life's just a joke with a few hidden fawns.'

In the vale where laughter runs free,
Every creature sings its own harmony.
With love and absurdity woven tight,
In the vibrant world, it's always delight.

Harbingers of the Harvest Moon

In the garden, pumpkins dance,
They spin and twirl, in a trance.
Cabbages giggle, what a show!
Corn crows laugh, "We're the stars, you know!"

Squirrels in pajamas take a stroll,
Chasing each other, that's their role.
Carrots wear hats, quite the sight,
Even the beets think they're all right.

The moon peeks through, with a grin,
Mischievous shadows begin to spin.
Goblins sneak treats, oh what a plot,
While ghosts munch snacks, why not?

Under the stars, fun does bloom,
With laughs and giggles, plenty of room.
Harvest night brings joy to all,
Even the owls hear the call.

Whispers of Windswept Wishes

In the breeze, a kite goes high,
It zigzags left as it sweeps by.
String gets tangled, oh what a mess!
"Who tied that knot?" the wind can guess!

Leaves are chatting in a huff,
"Who brought the acorns? That's too tough!"
While clouds giggle, floating so light,
They wear the sun like a silly bright.

Dandelions fluff up for their turn,
Telling secrets while fires burn.
A butterfly joins, flaps with flair,
Saying, "Let's dance without a care!"

Wishes float on giggles too,
In the fun of this wild rendezvous.
So chase your dreams, let laughter win,
For joy's a friend, let's dive right in!

Murmurs of Melancholy in the Mist

Fog rolls in, quite the sneaky plan,
Hiding the garden and old man Stan.
He trips on roses, a twist and shout,
While crickets chuckle, "What's that about?"

A lonely scarecrow sighs in vain,
His crows are off on a wild campaign.
"Who needs a friend when you've got style?"
He strikes a pose, has a cheeky smile.

A cat on a fence gives a big yawn,
Says, "Why do all these shrubs look drawn?"
Yet mischief swirls in the heavy air,
As owls join in to make a pair.

In the mist, laughter skips a beat,
Even the shadows have light on their feet.
So sigh not deeply, lift your chin,
For joy and shadows both can win!

Resounding Rhythms of Rustling Leaves

Leaves are drumming, what a beat,
Tap dancing squirrels join the street.
With acorns falling like little drums,
Nature's got rhythm, oh how it hums!

Wind plays the flute, soft and low,
While tree trunks dance, putting on a show.
Branches wave like they're in sync,
"Come on, friend, let's all link!"

The fox trots by, prancing with flair,
Wearing a scarf like a true millionaire.
Chasing his tail, he takes a bow,
"Is this a party? I'll join, wow!"

In this forest, the fun won't cease,
As laughter swirls, bringing peace.
Tune your heart to nature's song,
In laughter's arms, you can't go wrong!

Beneath the Ancient Boughs

Squirrels dance, a silly sight,
Chasing tails in morning light.
Branches shake with laughter's sound,
In this leafy kingdom found.

Beneath the boughs, we share a snack,
A picnic spread—a friendly pack.
But ants, oh my! They join the spree,
A tiny army, none agree!

The bark's a canvas for some art,
A smiley face, a joyful heart.
Nature giggles, windswept beams,
As we weave our silly dreams.

Beneath these branches, we all play,
Making mischief day by day.
Laughter echoes, leaves reply,
In this grove, who needs to fly?

Reflections in the Rippling Stream

A mirror lies 'neath willow trees,
With fish that giggle, if you please.
They wiggle tales, both big and small,
As water whispers, 'Come and sprawl!'

Not far away, a frog sings loud,
A croaky joke to gather crowd.
The ducks quack back, they're in on fun,
A feathered squad, no need to run.

With splashes bright, the sun does play,
On silver ripples, all the day.
Here laughter dances on the breeze,
Tickling ears and bending knees.

Reflections tease, and nature's jest,
In playful waters, we feel our best.
What tales we'll spin, as shadows gleam,
In this place, we live the dream.

Legends of the Leaf-strewn Lane

Beneath the leaves, we tiptoe round,
Searching for the laughs we found.
A treasure map? Just a clue,
To muffins baked with giggly stew.

A toadstool throne for royalty rare,
With bugs as subjects—what a scare!
Their tiny crowns, so out of place,
Yet every bug has a funny face.

Legends live where shadows curl,
In laughter's dance, the leaves unfurl.
Whispers float on breezy trails,
As we recount our wacky tales.

A squirrel's quest, a noble deed,
To hide acorns, yes indeed!
Along this lane, our spirits soar,
Each leaf a laugh, who could want more?

The Lost Songs of Autumn

A chorus of crunch beneath our feet,
As leaves dance down, oh what a treat!
They sway and swirl, a funny ballet,
In autumn's breeze, we laugh and play.

With pumpkins grinning from their spots,
They whisper jokes, forget-me-nots.
Witches cackle on their brooms,
While goblins plot in leafy rooms.

A songbird flies with silly flair,
Singing tunes without a care.
But what's this? A lost refrain,
A melody that brings the rain!

Autumn's symphony, bright and clear,
With giggles layered, loud and near.
In every rustle, every gust,
Lies laughter shared, a joyful trust.

The Past Between the Leaves

Once a squirrel tried to be a chef,
He made acorn soup but lost his bet.
The recipe flew high in the breeze,
Now woodland critters demand their cheese!

A wise old owl, with spectacles tight,
Claimed he'd teach mice to dance at night.
But they tripped on tails, made such a scene,
The show was wild—oh, what a dream!

A rabbit once wore a fancy bow tie,
Said he'd impress the butterflies nearby.
He hopped and spun, but fell with a thud,
The flowers laughed—what a show of mud!

A turtle rolled in a game of tag,
Said he was fast, but it made us gag.
In a slow-motion chase, he took a dive,
Seems he preferred the calm of jive!

Murmurs in the Twilight

In the twilight, the frogs began to croak,
Their rhythm was silly, what a hoax!
A neighbor complained, 'Keep it down back there!'
The crickets just laughed, saying life's unfair.

A hedgehog sat sipping his herbal tea,
Chatting with fireflies—quite fancy, you see.
He said, 'Oh dear, my spines do ache,'
They giggled and formed a sparkly lake.

The wind whistled tunes of forgotten jokes,
While raccoons played charades with old folks.
With winks and nods, they acted so sly,
Even the moon would roll by and sigh.

Beneath a tree, a dance-off began,
With turtles and beetles leading the plan.
Round and round, oh what a sight,
Mirth ruled the night, oh, what a delight!

Shadows Under the Boughs

In the shadows, a squirrel wore shades,
Declared himself king in many parades.
"Bow down!" he squeaked, with his acorn crown,
But the ants just giggled and dusted the ground.

A wise old fox pulled a prank on the hare,
He hid their snacks under the cool, dark lair.
When found, they laughed till their stomachs hurt,
The game was grand, oh, how they flirt!

There once was a tree with a laugh quite loud,
It asked if the clouds were feeling proud.
With each roll of thunder, it shook with glee,
"Make way for rain, I'm as funny as can be!"

A group of mice threw a grand little feast,
With crumbs for the birds, they invited the beast.
The owl got lost in a maze of cheese,
Tickled, they swayed, saying, "More, if you please!"

Reflections on the Forest Floor

On the forest floor, a picnic laid wide,
Bears hawked the goods while the rabbits did hide.
'Best carrot cake!' they proudly declared,
While raccoons snuck bites—oh, how they shared!

A lizard in shades posed like a star,
Claimed he was famous—was he, by far?
A snail held the mic, ready to flow,
"Tales of the slowest—come watch my show!"

Mice spun stories of adventures gone wrong,
In the shade of the leaves, singing their song.
"The world's quite big, beyond this green realm,
But here, with friends, we're taken by helm."

With laughter and light spreading round like cheer,
The forest rang out, the mood was so clear.
And so we all danced, in the shine of the sun,
As long as we're together, we'll always have fun!

Tales Carved in Timber

In the woods, the squirrels giggle,
As they scamper and dance, oh what a wriggle!
The trees wear hats made of moss and cheer,
Whispering secrets that only they hear.

A woodpecker drums a silly tune,
Chasing shadows beneath the moon.
Branches shake as a raccoon prances,
Nature's circus: come see their dances!

Frogs in tuxedos, polished and neat,
Practicing for their grand, green retreat.
While owls hoot in a playful jest,
Wondering which critter is dancing best.

With acorns tossed like confetti high,
And playful winds that tease and sigh.
Laughter rings in the forest deep,
Where whimsical dreams are free to leap.

The Echoing Heart of the Woods

In the heart of green, there's a funny sound,
As squirrels argue who's taller, who's round!
Raccoons read newspapers, face serious,
While birds gossip wildly, oh so curious!

A turtle in shades strolls quite slow,
Thinking he's the star of the woodland show.
The frogs croak their own version of rap,
As fireflies flicker, they dance on the map!

A deer wears a bowtie, brings style to the place,
Bouncing not far, just keeping their pace.
The laughter of leaves in a playful breeze,
Turns the forest into a comedic tease.

When night falls, the critters collide,
In a comedy club where giggles reside.
With mushrooms as stools and starlight for stage,
The woodland's delightful—turning every page!

Chasing Sunbeams Through Branches

Chasing rays of light, oh what a sight,
The rabbits play tag, hopping left and right.
Chipmunks roll acorns like bowling balls,
In this playful paradise, goofy laughter calls!

A breeze rustles leaves, tickling the ground,
A bear tries to dance, but just spins around.
Hilarity reigns in this tree-bound race,
With a wily coyote making silly face!

Sunbeams peek down, casting silly shapes,
While a group of frogs practice for leaps and escapes.
The rush of the wind carries merry tunes,
As nature's stand-up unfolds under moons!

Joyful echoes resonate, a laughter spree,
In a world where giggles are wild and free.
So come join the chase, where fun never ends,
And sunlight invites all the woodland friends!

Laments of the Lost Pines

Once proud and tall, now a bit askew,
The pines share their tales, a quirky view.
With sap-soaked stories and knots of delight,
They chuckle at wind's playful slight!

'Once I had needles, look at me now!'
Said a tree with a spin, looking quite proud.
While squirrels snicker, in coats all askew,
Pranking their pals with a sticky gum glue!

The owls wear glasses, trying to see,
The antics of critters as funny as can be.
With bark that can crack in a giggling burst,
Nature's own jesters, quenching their thirst.

In the twilight glow, the pines still stand tall,
Sharing their laughter, inviting us all.
So listen closely to their chuckles and sighs,
For even the lost can find joy in the skies!

Reverberations of Rustic Dreams

In a barn, the rooster sings,
But it sounds more like a cat with springs.
The cows are dancing, quite a sight,
While pigs in tutus twirl with delight.

Grasshoppers hold a talent show,
Even frogs have started to throw!
With every ribbit, they claim their fame,
While crickets all clap, it's quite the game.

A goat on stilts struts with flair,
While chickens gossip without a care.
The wind whispers tales of silly pranks,
As the barnyard crew gives their thanks.

So here we laugh in fields so wide,
Where dreamers roam with joy and pride.
In the rural realm, we can't compete,
With creatures making their own heartbeat.

Leafy Legends in Twilight

A squirrel in shades made its debut,
Claiming the acorns—a rich little cue.
With each leap and bound just like a star,
Deserving of trophies, he's our top czar.

Old trees whisper tales of their youth,
Of sapling romances and toothy tooth.
The owls hold court, wise with delight,
As critters gather beneath moonlight.

Beneath a branch, a raccoon will jest,
With jokes that put all others to rest.
The fireflies dance, twinkling their glee,
While leaves applaud in rustling spree.

So let us frolic in the dusk's embrace,
With legends and laughter, a warm-hearted place.
Where every rustle is laced with a grin,
And the night is a party where fun always wins.

The Winding Path of Remembrance

On a winding way, I stumbled and tripped,
Chasing my thoughts, my memory slipped.
But a wise old turtle just chuckled and said,
"Take it slow, my friend, don't rush your head!"

A signpost grinned, cheeky and bright,
"Lost your way? Well, isn't that right!"
I laughed out loud at this playful spark,
While bees buzzed by like confetti in the park.

A jolly old man painted signs with flair,
"Go left for laughs, or right for despair!"
A squirrel commented with a twinkle and laugh,
"Whichever you choose, you'll still need a map!"

In moments of mischief, I found my way,
Through paths of giggles and games to play.
For every stumble down this twisty route,
Leads to laughter that wears no suit.

Murmuring Mists in the Meadow

In a meadow where mists weave and play,
A field mouse declared, "Let's have a parade!"
With cheery fox hats and carrots so bright,
They tiptoed around, misty creatures in flight.

A rabbit suggested they dance in style,
Doing the jitters with giggles and smiles.
While owls looked on, their hoots full of cheer,
Mystified by antics they'd not seen here.

Butterflies twirled, with colors that shone,
While clovers all gathered to join in the fun.
A wise old crow laughed, perched up on high,
"Who knew fog could dance and make spirits fly?"

So in swirling mists, laughter echoes wide,
With friendships cherished that none can divide.
In this meadow of magic, we skip without care,
Where whispers of joy dance in the air.

The Enigma of Twisted Branches

In the woods where shadows play,
Squirrels gossip night and day,
A raccoon steals a picnic feast,
While owls laugh, a raucous beast.

Branches twist like stories told,
With every quirk, a prank unfolds,
A squirrel wearing a tiny hat,
Cackles loudly, "Hey, look at that!"

Beneath the trees, a dance begins,
With mushrooms joining in the spins,
A frog croaks jokes that make you cheer,
The forest floor becomes a pier.

Mossy carpets catch you off guard,
As critters play solitaire hard,
In trunks, the woodpeckers drum,
Echoing tales, both silly and glum.

Secrets of the Whispering Woods

Cicadas buzz a tune so spry,
While fireflies wink as they fly by,
A hedgehog wears a feather plume,
Claiming it's his hat of gloom.

The bushes chuckle with delight,
As shadows prance in the moonlight,
A gnome with shoes of mismatched flair,
Trips on roots, oh, how they stare!

The trees conspire with glee in rhymes,
Telling tales of clumsy times,
A fox in shades pretends to read,
Liberating laughter with speed.

Whispers tell of all the fun,
Jokes that rival a well-aimed pun,
In this realm of frolic and cheer,
Nature's mirth is crystal clear.

Tapestry of Gnarled Roots

Beneath the surface, roots entwine,
In a dance that's simply benign,
Rabbits play peek-a-boo, oh so sly,
While turtles laugh as they stroll by.

The tangled tales that roots can weave,
Of tree-based shenanigans, hard to believe,
A hedgehog shoes a tiny sk8r,
Performing tricks—what a creator!

In every knot, a story hides,
Within the bark, the humor bides,
Mice tell stories of cheese divine,
As their visions of grandeur align.

The roots all root for silly dreams,
Like saplings racing down the streams,
With laughter echoing through the bark,
They cheer until the bright sparks dark.

The Sigh of the Aging Land

The ground creaks softly, tales retold,
Of mischief somewhat uncontrolled,
A rabbit hops on a ghostly line,
Chasing shadows that twist and twine.

The stones chuckle as they sit still,
Watching frights that give a thrill,
A wanderer trips, an elegant fowl,
Shouts of laughter, a great big growl.

Trees whisper secrets among the leaves,
Of past haunts the forest weaves,
A squirrel hoards pranks for the day,
Planning each one in the funniest way.

Through every sigh, a chuckle flows,
In the heart of woods where wonder glows,
The aging land is young at heart,
With every laugh, it plays its part.

Timeless Trails Through Shaded Paths

Beneath the boughs, I stumble and sway,
Chasing squirrels, while they laugh and play.
The sun sneaks in, but I still can't see,
Where my wandering thoughts just might be.

A dog appears with a frisbee in tow,
I think he's got more sense than I know.
Chasing my shadow, I trip on a root,
Just another mess in this woodland suit!

Trees whisper secrets, or so it appears,
While leaves tumble down like my childish fears.
What's that? A rustle? Is it a deer?
Nope, just a raccoon, and I'm filled with cheer!

So onward I trek, funny fate at my side,
On trails that twist, where giggles collide.
The forest is laughing, with joy so absurd,
In this timeless dance, every joy is conferred.

The Lullaby of Hidden Glens

In hidden glens where the daisies bloom,
I trip on the roots, and then I resume.
A frog breaks the silence with a loud croak,
As if to say, 'Hey, don't let it provoke!'

A butterfly flutters, oh what a sight,
I wave at it softly, we're both taking flight.
Under the canopy, life's funny parade,
Moments like this are never delayed!

A picnic begins with a sandwich that flies,
The raccoons are stealthy and cunning, oh my!
They dance on the blanket, they nibble, they munch,
With crumbs on my shirt, I feel like a hunch!

As sunlight departs with a wink and a grin,
I gather my treasures, this day's such a win!
The glens sing a tune so light and absurd,
In laughter, I find my heart's greatest word.

Pine-Scented Reminiscence

In the pine-scented air, I find my delight,
With squirrels in tuxedos, what a funny sight!
They scurry and scamper, planning a coup,
Just to swipe snacks from my picnic stew.

The trees seem to chuckle at my clumsy feet,
With branches that low five, such a warm greet!
A bee buzzes in, like it owns the whole place,
I run from the buzz, but oh, what a race!

A chipmunk looks up with a cheeky little grin,
It snatches my cookie, and I'm left with a wince.
Yet somehow I laugh, this day's like a play,
With nature's cast making my worries decay.

As dusk paints the sky, I wave my goodbyes,
To the prankster brigade beneath twilight skies.
In every sweet moment, it's laughter I find,
In the pine-scented tales left behind.

Nature's Unwritten Chronicles

The chronicles of trees whisper tales of jest,
Of squirrels in leggings, and birds on a quest.
Each crack of a twig holds comedy's right,
While I trip on a root, what a hilarious night!

A hedgehog ambles, with all of its might,
Searching for snacks under stars shining bright.
I stumble beside it, we both lose our way,
But his armor's robust; I'm the one in dismay!

The creek sings a song, unplanned but so grand,
As frogs form a choir, their talents unplanned.
With laughter contagious, I'm rolling with glee,
As nature's pen strokes the jokes just for me.

In the end, as the fireflies start to twirl,
I gather my thoughts, let spontaneity swirl.
For every adventure, there's fun intertwined,
In nature's great book, this chapter's divine!

Burdened by the Blowing Breeze

The wind sways trees, a quirky sight,
Branches dance funny, oh what a fright!
A squirrel holds tight on a branch so high,
Thinking it's flying, oh my, oh my!

Leaves whirl around like a playful prank,
Rustling and fussing, no time to thank.
A hat takes a trip, with a twist and a twirl,
Chasing a breeze, it just might unfurl.

Nature's own jest, in a breezy parade,
A game of tag where no one's delayed.
Watch out for the gusts, they sneak up to tease,
They tickle your ears with their ticklish breezes.

So laugh at the antics, let your worries cease,
A lighthearted dance in the playful peace.
When the air gets a chuckle, don't be forlorn,
Join in the frolic, it's just a breeze born!

Sighs of Soughing Winds

The winds come whispering, soft, and slow,
  Muttering secrets that no one can know.
A gust sneezes loudly, a raucous surprise,
  Leaves scatter wildly, like startled spies.

Wandering about with a flimsy intent,
They tug at your shirt, it's a cheeky event.
  A flurry of giggles and playful shouts,
As the breeze plays tag with forgotten doubts.

With every soft sigh, a joke falls in place,
  A tickle of laughter, a flip of your face.
If winds could but talk, oh the tales they'd weave,
  Of playful pranks, in a world we believe.

So next time it blows, just take off your frown,
  Dance with the gales, wear a leafy crown.
For in every murmur, a chuckle is found,
  Even the soughing can turn life around!

The Ageless Dance of Seasons

Spring hops around with a skipping sway,
Bunnies and blossoms join in the play.
Summer struts in with a bright sunny grin,
Ice cream drips down, oh where to begin?

Autumn arrives with a crunch and a swirl,
Spinning leaves down, giving colors a twirl.
While winter grumbles, all snuggled in white,
Snowmen make faces, what a silly sight!

Each season a dancer, with quirks of their own,
A trail of good humor wherever they've flown.
They giggle and tumble, in nature's ballet,
Transforming our world in a luminous way.

So celebrate changes, don't let them intrude,
Join in the dance, a jubilant mood.
In laughter and cycles, we all can partake,
For life's an adventure, make no mistake!

Petals in the Pathway

Petals start falling, a colorful show,
A soft pink carpet where giggly feet go.
But watch your step, for they start to slide,
A comical tumble on a whimsical ride.

The path is alive with a brilliant array,
Where daisies and roses all laugh and play.
A bee buzzes by, with a hum and a grin,
"Excuse me!" it says, "Let the fun begin!"

A flurry of petals caught up in the breeze,
Dancing around us, without any ease.
They swirl in the air like confetti in flight,
Turning a dull day into sheer delight.

So step lightly, friends, in this garden of cheer,
For laughter abounds when the petals draw near.
In the whimsical waltz of bright blossoms free,
Find joy in the journey, just smile and be!

Songs of the Solitary Sparrow

A sparrow sits upon a wire,
With dreams as big as they aspire.
In his tiny beak, a crumb he holds,
Sings of adventures, both brave and bold.

His friends all chirp from near and far,
But he insists he's the best by far.
With a puffed-up chest, he steals the show,
While others just watch his one-man show.

Each morning he tries a brand new tune,
Though most just sound like a silly croon.
But to the heart, he brings delight,
As he flaps his wings and takes to flight.

In the evening quiet, he spins a yarn,
Of fights with cats and a time of charm.
Little does he know, that he's adored,
A solo star, forever floored!

The Retreat of the Setting Sun

The sun bows down behind the hill,
With a wink and nod, what a thrill!
It paints the sky in shades of gold,
While crickets sing tales untold.

A lazy cat sprawls on the ground,
Dreams of chasing shadows abound.
The sun chuckles, 'Oh, what a sight!
Tomorrow, I'll be back—hold tight!'

Bats take flight with a playful swoop,
While birds are settling in their group.
They gossip and giggle through the trees,
As the sun ducks out with a gentle breeze.

All creatures pause as darkness falls,
The night's soft laughter gently calls.
With stars that twinkle, the stage is set,
For a cosmic dance we shan't forget!

Dappled Light on the Forest Floor

Little beams that dance and play,
On lush green leaves where critters stay.
The shadows stretch, the colors mix,
As squirrels plot their nutty tricks.

Sunlight flickers, a game of hide,
As bunnies bounce and take the stride.
A fox tiptoes, with mischief planned,
While mushrooms laugh at the silly band.

A squirrel trips over a fallen log,
Turns to laugh with an oversized frog.
Together they roll, a comic scene,
Nature's stage where fun's routine.

In this dappled realm, all jokes apply,
Each leaf whispers secrets as days go by.
When the sun sets, they'll tell the tale,
Of woodland mischief beneath the veil!

Stories of the Swaying Sycamore

Beneath the big sycamore's arms,
The breeze weaves tales with quirky charms.
Its branches sway, a storyteller bold,
Sharing secrets from days of old.

The leaves giggle with every breeze,
Ticking away like a clock at ease.
Children gather, eyes open wide,
As the sycamore shares its leafy pride.

A raccoon nods, munching on a snack,
While fireflies flash with laughter in the back.
The sycamore sways, its laughter loud,
Embracing all, growing ever proud.

As twilight wraps the world in night,
The sycamore twinkles, a soothing sight.
With each rustle, the stories flow,
In this magical place where laughter grows!

Myths of the Mulberry Meadow

In a field where mulberries grow,
Bumblebees dance with a silly show.
A squirrel stole a young child's hat,
Now it wears it like a dapper brat.

The gossiping grasshoppers chirp with glee,
Claiming the moon sings in their spree.
A rabbit tripped on a stick of wood,
Then laughed and said, "This can't be good!"

The daisies gossip, not shy at all,
About a frog who thinks he's tall.
He jumps and lands on a poor old snail,
Who just sighed and went back to the trail.

As the sun sets with a giggle and grin,
The shadows of mischief begin to spin.
In the meadow where laughter's enslaved,
Each tale feels like a good-humored wave.

Shadows Under the Swaying Spruce

Beneath a spruce, there's a shadowy dance,
Where boots and socks often lose the chance.
A raccoon steals an unsuspecting shoe,
While the old owl hoots, "What to do?"

The squirrels chat about nutty dreams,
Of acorns floating down in streams.
One mocks a chipmunk for choosing wrong,
Claiming he's humming a nutty song.

When the breeze whistles tunes from above,
The pinecones giggle, it's a true love.
They twirl and spin as the branches sway,
In their own funky, forest ballet.

With laughter loud, they drop to the ground,
Each chuckle ticking like a fun-filled sound.
In shadows deep where the humor grows,
Life's quirks pop up like a garden of prose.

Lanterns of Luminous Memories

In a dark room where laughter ignites,
Lanterns flicker with glowing delights.
A cat in a hat sings with a crow,
While the stuffed bears put on a show.

Balloons giggle as they brush the wall,
Teasing the frisbee that's bound to fall.
They scheme and dream of a wild balloon,
Floating off to light up the moon.

A puppy, dressed sharp in a tiny vest,
Tries to impress the friendly quest.
But trips on the rug, oh what a sight,
Lands on a cupcake that glows so bright!

Each memory colors the room's delight,
With tales that twinkle like stars at night.
In a place where joys never cease,
Laughter enchants and madness finds peace.

Traces of Time Through Twisted Roots

The trees have secrets wrapped in their bark,
Whispers of fables sung after dark.
A turtle claimed it was once a hare,
But his slow stroll tells a different affair.

Worms slither safely beneath the soil,
Giggling away from the sun's warm toil.
They boast of races they'd surely win,
If only the bunnies would let them begin.

Twisted roots hold tales from long ago,
Where missteps and giggles have room to grow.
A raccoon in sunglasses, looking quite sly,
Cracks jokes with a juniper, aiming high.

As shadows lengthen and the sun bids adieu,
The spirits of laughter stir up the dew.
In a dance that's silly, depicted with cheer,
Time's sly humor whispers, "Just lend an ear!"

Shadows on the Old Trail

Beneath the trees where squirrels play,
I tripped on roots, what a clumsy display.
The shadows laughed, 'Do take a seat!'
But I bounced back up—quite light on my feet.

A raccoon peeked from behind a post,
I swear it looked like it laughed the most.
With twinkling eyes and a cheeky grin,
I could almost hear it say, "Let's begin!"

Footprints danced on the dirt ahead,
Only to find a deer who fled.
"Don't run!" I fumbled, trying to call,
While slipping and sliding, I took a fall.

The shadows murmured tales of yore,
While I sat there, stuck, wanting more.
In the twilight's giggle, we all conspire,
As old trails share laughter, never tire.

Flickers of Light Through the Branches

Sunbeams wiggle like a fizzy drink,
They tease the leaves, no time to think.
Like disco balls in the forest's dance,
I tried to boogie, but had no chance.

A chipmunk jived, all puffy and spry,
I joined in quickly, oh me, oh my!
With a little groove and a silly spin,
We laughed so hard, my head went thin.

Through branches swayed, neon glow warmed,
While I tried to sip from nature's charm.
But bees had opinions on who was the best,
Their buzzing hum made me feel like a pest.

Yet the flickers winked, "Keep moving, friend!"
As lights above whispered, "This is not the end!"
With every quirk and twist of fate,
We danced 'til dusk—oh, isn't life great?

Secrets Hidden in the Underbrush

Whispers of laughter, a secret delight,
A hedgehog rolled in a curious fight.
Beneath the ferns, a party ensued,
With all the creatures, merry and rude.

A ladybug lost in a game of hide,
While ants marched on, filled with much pride.
"Find the snack!" the hedgehog declared,
As we all searched 'round, none of us scared.

A slippery worm said, "I'm the best treat!"
But a frog croaked back, "You can't be beat!"
Legs in the air, a dance of debate,
Who's the true winner? We fumbled with fate.

Through tales and giggles among the bramble,
Where secrets linger, the wild folks ramble.
With laughter and mischief, our hearts intertwined,
In nature's embrace, pure joy we find.

The Sweet Sigh of Summer's End

As the leaves turned gold, the breeze whispered soft,
I spotted a cat, somersaulting aloft.
"Cats don't fly!" I laughed with delight,
But there it soared, oh what a sight!

The sun was sluggish, taking a rest,
While the crickets chirped, they knew what's best.
"Hold tight!" I yelled to the fruit-flying pears,
As they rolled past my limbs, uncombed hair.

With each golden hour, the laughter would swell,
Who knew summer could be such a sell?
Yet autumn danced in, wearing her crown,
Shaking her head at my antics' renown.

The sweet sigh of change, with a wink and a cheer,
Nature's last giggle, just before the year.
As shadows lengthen and days start to bend,
We'll laugh through it all, my quirky friend.

The Grove's Silent Secrets

In the grove where whispers play,
Squirrels steal the food all day.
Mice debate on who is bold,
While shadows dance, tales are told.

Frogs in coats of slimy green,
Discussing where the flies have been.
Wobbly turtles race with glee,
Giving the rabbits quite a spree.

Breezes giggle through the leaves,
Tickling branches that time retrieves.
Old branches creak with laughter's sound,
As secrets spin and twirl around.

Here, the humor softly peeks,
Nature's jesters hide in streaks.
With every rustle, jest comes new,
In the grove where mirth ensues.

Treetop Murmurs at Dusk

At dusk the tree tops start to chat,
An owl's tired voice heaves like a bat.
Owls trade jokes about the moon,
While crickets serenade a tune.

Leafy figures whisper low,
When passing clouds begin to glow.
A raccoon wears a mask so sly,
Stealing snacks as stars drift by.

Branches jive, swaying to funk,
A dance-off to shake off the junk.
Squirrels break out in acrobatics,
Turning leaves into gymnastic antics.

Through the night, the trees conspire,
To share their tales that never tire.
With every whisper comes a grin,
As the giggles in the treetops spin.

Memories Among the Bark

Among the bark, old stories cling,
Of beetles dancing and frogs that sing.
Roots are plotting a mystery plan,
While ants march in a silly band.

Woodpeckers tap a beat so sweet,
Like drummers keeping time to greet.
Foxes chuckle at a broken twig,
While owls host mystery, big and big.

Peeking raccoons steal the show,
As laughter ripples to and fro.
Even the flowers seem to sway,
To the forest's upbeat play.

A dance of shadows, night-time fun,
Every creature joins; the jam's begun.
In this bark-bound comedy fair,
Laughter sparkles in the air.

Fables from the Forest Floor

Beneath the trees, tales intertwine,
Where worms weave stories just divine.
Rabbits overflow with giggly quips,
While ladybugs take funny trips.

Ants prepare their feast with flair,
Chasing crumbs with utmost care.
Frogs on logs swap silly glares,
While whispering breezes tousle hairs.

Mushrooms gossip in colors bright,
Turning every shade into delight.
Sass from the shadows, a critter's play,
In every corner, jests parade.

As twilight drapes the wood's embrace,
Each story brings a smiling face.
On the forest floor, it's all about cheer,
Where laughter echoes loud and clear.

Beneath the Arching Canopy

The branches wave like silly hands,
As squirrels plot their playful plans.
"Look! A nut!" one shouts and dives,
But misses me—oh, what a jive!

The shadows dance, they twist and turn,
A light show, oh how they burn!
The sun peeks through, a golden cheat,
I trip on roots beneath my feet!

The birds chirp jokes in harmony,
About the acorn's lost journey.
Laughter fills the cooling air,
As I mix up my own despair!

So come on down, join in the fun,
Beneath this arch, the day is won.
We'll laugh and play 'til shadows flee,
In this woodland, wild and free!

Songs of the Silent Trees

The trees are singing, but can you hear?
Oh wait, that's just a woodpecker near!
He's tapping tunes on bark so grand,
While a raccoon leads the funky band.

A breeze joins in with a whoosh and sway,
"Dance with me!" the leaves would say.
But one fell down, took a comical spin,
And landed right on the turtle's chin.

The branches giggle, swaying low,
As critters share their best hello.
A hedgehog juggles acorns galore,
While a rabbit jumps through a funny door!

So gather 'round in nature's groove,
With every twist, there's room to move.
Let's join the trees in laughter's spree,
They're singing songs just for you and me!

The Dance of Leaves in Autumn's Embrace

Leaves are twirling, like they just can't stop,
In a whirl of colors, who knows where they'll flop?
A leaf went high, then lost its race,
And landed smack on a dog's wet face!

"Oh please," said him, "not another prank!"
While squirrels laugh from their lofty plank.
They toss down twigs, they're feeling bold,
Creating chaos, oh so uncontrolled!

The acorns roll, like bowling balls,
As nature plays its funny calls.
A chipmunk slips and takes a dive,
In a pile of leaves, oh what a vibe!

So let the dance continue on,
As autumn sings its silly song.
We'll join the laughter, high and free,
In this land of humor and glee!

Whispers in the Woodland Mist

The mist is creeping like a shy cat,
As I sneeze, the squirrels say, "What's that?"
They giggle low, point their little paws,
While I check for ghosts—oh, what a cause!

Strange shadows move, I can't set my gaze,
Is that just fog or a funny craze?
A toad hops up, "You scaredy cat!"
I do a twirl; "Let's dance with that!"

The fog thickens, but in a fun way,
And creatures come out to join the play.
A fox declares, "Let's hide and seek!"
As water drops from the trees, they squeak!

So come, my friend, let's share a laugh,
In this woodland's quirky, funny path.
With every whisper, the jokes will bloom,
In this mist that fills the quiet room!

www.ingramcontent.com/pod-product-compliance
Lightning Source LLC
Chambersburg PA
CBHW071847160426
43209CB00003B/454